Whose Reflection is That

ROBIN TAYLOR

Copyright © 2018 by Robin Taylor
All rights reserved. No part of this book may be reproduced, scanned,
or distributed in any printed or electronic form without permission.
First Edition: November 2018
Printed in the United States of America
ISBN-13: 9781642542219 PB
ISBN-13: 9781645500087 HB

Table of Contents

Hidden Truth 1
Wrong FIT 3
Advice 4
Fragile Dawn 6
Guiding Light 9
Crest of a Wave 11
Desire to be heard 13
Hidden Away 15
Star lit Dream 17
Awkward Encounter 19
Scattered Dreams 20
Mote of Dust 21
Society Is A Shadow 22
Lost Dreams 24
Double Standards 26
A Path Misled 28
Safety in the Darkness 29
Crowded Conversation 30
Destructive Dreams 32
Train of Conversation 34
Normal Life 36
A Day Best Forgotten 39
Misused 40
In My Shoes 41
Journey's Path 42
Diamond in Disguise 43
Dreams and Wishes 45

Hidden Truth

Our faces often
Hide who
We really are,

For those with
Disorders this
Can be a devastating
CURSE!

For underneath
Our normal exterior,
We are different,

Often playful
At the wrong time,
Mouth saying
The wrong thing
At the wrong time,

Mood changes when
Others perceive
There should be
No reason why,

Thumping hearts,
Sweaty palms,
Shallow breath,
Light headedness,

Feeling a crushing
Force
Ever present
Ready to strike,

We are not dumb
Stupid
Moronic
Or retarded,
We can't help
Being as we are,

Being born
Different is hard
To deal with
On a daily basis,

It is made even harder
With pre-judgment
Made against
Those such as us,

So, what you can do
Is ease up!
Let us live in peace
As we do for you.

Wrong FIT

He is not the same.
Who's to blame?
Because he's not the same.

Pushed to the side,
Prodded and poked.

Bring out mould 6,
That should do the trick.
OH NO!
He's not the same.

Now 23 and 32,
Didn't fit him at all,
What a shame.

Bring out,
General fit 42,
That one should fit you,
Like a trick.

DAMN!
DAMN!
DAMMIT!

This is quite
INSANE,
He is not the same!

Advice

Advice comes in many forms
From those you know
To those unknown.

Friendly advice is wonderful
But can lead to trouble
If you are not careful.

Some advice comes
From years of experience.

Then there are those
Who parrot
What they have heard
With little or no
Understanding of what
They are saying.

It can get very hard
To know what advice
To take on board.

From good advice,
Can come riches
Contentment and self-worth.

From bad advice
Disaster and low self esteem
Awaits.

The Choice is yours

May you find,
The right one for you.

Fragile Dawn

Wake up to a day too bright
Something doesn't
Seem quite right

Birds are LOUD
And what IS that SMELL

Several shirts later
Wearing my best
Most comfortable one
Still too itchy
Not quite as bad
As the rest.

Eye brows and lashes
Are twitching and itching
Need to pull them out
For some relief

Sudden movement
Out the corner
Of my eye

Turn to look
Nothing but a shadow
On the wall moving by

Walk into a room
The light flickered
A hand pushed
My head....
But no one is there

Mood is unstable
Dusty feeling on my hands
CAN'T keep them clean

Someone shouts
In normal tones
Need to exit fast
From this very noisy room

Over reaction
To the mildest thing
Is very hard to fight
The world is getting
Very crazy

I have come to realize that
On these day'sI am having
What I have come to call
A heightened Aspie day

It can be frustrating, Confusing
And sometimes scary
This comes on with no thought
Or planning

It is non-curable
Can last for a few hours
Or a few days

All I can do is
HIDE and hope
I don't upset
The surrounding
Natural balance
Of life.

Guiding Light

When I fall
From the path of life
And I lose my way,

When the darkness of life
Catches up with me,

When the baying creatures
That live in the darkness
Ever beckon me to join
Their weird wild world,

There is one sure thing,

You are the light
That guides me home
When I have lost my way….

I often stumble and fall
Through life's bumpy journey,

Just when life
Is at its lowest point,

You appear
To help guide me
Back to the right path,

I am forever grateful
For all you have done
And if ever you are in need
Of a guiding light
I will always be there for you.

Crest of a Wave

I ride life on
The crest of a wave
Never seeming to
Catch up with the
New or old schools
Of life.

When the wave
Starts to fade
I find myself
Surrounded by
A glass brick wall.

Unable to move
To where I can see
I need to be
This is very frustrating
And hard to deal with.

I can't even reach out
To those on the other side
Of the glass brick wall
As I seem to be invisible
To all that surrounds me.

So caught up in their own
Self-important little world
That I go unnoticed
Even when my world
Is crumbling around me.

Though when I stumble
And fall
Like a wrecking ball
They react.

The world takes notice
And I suffer the
Wrath of the ones
Who think they
KNOW ALL.

Desire to be heard

Jumbled words
Flow freely
From his lips
Of this there
Is no doubt

Verbal conversation
Is in doubt

He doesn't see things
Very straight
From unclouded vision
The world is a blur

His brain doesn't
Compute the world
The way so called
Normal people do

Given time
Patience and understanding,
As others do receive,
His words will
Unjumble for
All the world to hear.

His vision will clear
As the world opens to him.

His head will rise.

Understanding turns
To smiles,
Smiles to hugs.
The grey cloud
Hanging above
His head
Will disappear.

Hidden Away

Why do you play computer games?
When you could be outside!
With your friends.

Playing sports or sitting
In a group in general conversation,
Or out meeting new people.

The answer is simple.

Games don't Hurt me!
Bully me!
Mock me!
Make fun!
Or Abuse me!

Where as in my games,
I can have fun in peace,
I can be anyone I want to be.

Just because they don't understand
What I am all about,
Does not give them the right
To make my life hell.

So, I hide away in my shell,
Inside my own bubble
Of happiness and safety
There is no physical hurt.

Years later I am still asked
Why I play games?
Rather than interact
With real people, outside.

Though I may be older
Nothing has changed.

Though I may not get physically
Hurt as often, it still hurts.
With all the misunderstanding,
Lack of knowledge and unacceptance,
Of who I really am.

It is hard to socialise
With all the prejudgement
Against one such as I.

Star lit Dream

As the stars
Come out tonight,
Your dreams
Start to wander.

Down a dark
And dusty path,
They almost
Seem to blunder.

As ghostly shadows
Dance and weave,
Amongst the
Darkened trees.

Whispers And sighs
Softly echo
Their lost
And forgotten dreams.

Some make you
Scream and
Run away to hide.

While others
Have you
Fall down laughing,

Yet others,
Are greeted
With a sigh,

This dusty path
Appears endless.

Time and again you try
To make sense,
Of what you are seeing.

This eclectic insanity,
Has your
Head spinning.

When you finally
Start to wake,
Words creep
From your lips,

What the hell
Was that all about!

As you drift of
Back to sleep.

Awkward Encounter

She smiles,
My heart
Skips a beat,
Soft words spoken,
My reply
Falters from my lips,
Mesmerised
By her looks,
Confusion,
Desperation,
Trying not to
Stumble
Or look the fool,

Aahhh!!

Words misspoken,
Too much to handle,
Losing control
Mouth in over drive,
Part company
Will see you
Around,
Days turn to
Months,

Encounter blown.

Scattered Dreams

Wafting dreams
Snare and delight,
My every waking hour.

The tricks they play
Throughout my day,
Mesmerise and delight.

I can fly away
With my dreams
All day and night.

But when I wake,
Reality comes
Flooding in.

They slip through
My fingers,
Like a tide in flight.

My dreams scatter
To the wind!

Mote of Dust

Like a speck of dust,
Drifting through eternity,
Unnoticed,
Unheard,
I drift right by,
Your vacant eye,
No acknowledgment,
No care,

A glimmer of hope,
As you turn my way,
But you walk right by,
Open a window,
The unforgiving wind,
Picks me up,
Blows me into
The dark night,

Into Oblivion!

Society Is A Shadow

To me society is
A huge daunting shadow
Murky blackness
And ink stained blotches
Surrounded by grey mist.

WHERE!!

Shadows dance and move
In erratic motion
That is hard to
Keep track of.

They dart in and out
Some come out and laugh
With hysterical giggles
And screeching.

Only to fade back
From whence they came.

Others emerge
To throw taunts
And jeers.

When my defences
Are at maximum.

One emerges to give
Comfort and hugs.

Defences are down,
And BAM!!
The shadows come back.

Lost Dreams

A once proud mirror
Lays broken and scattered
Across a dusty wooden floor.

Old foot prints weave
Endlessly around the shards
Ever intersecting.

A fading cry
From a nearby shard
Something moving.

Edging closer
Staring into the void
Grey mist meets your eye.

Shadows dance and weave
Fading into the mist
Future plans,
Lost dreams,
Greet your eye.

You stare in terror
As you come to realize
You have been here before.

You cringe away
As you come to realize
THE REFLECTIONS
ARE
YOU!

Double Standards

Double standards
Drive me crazy,
I always get
You MUST do this,
You MUST do that.

But when I ask
For a little in return,
All I usually get in reply,
I have not got the time
Or that is not the same

In return

Help me with this
And I will help you with that

WHAT A CROCK!!

OH, you will help me with
One little thing.
Won't you?

JUST THIS ONCE,
JUST THIS ONCE,
Over again.

I put up my hand
For a little help
All I get back is
I am too busy
Too help you now.

But what I can do
Is when you screw up!
Which we know you will do.

Like a wrecking ball
We will come down
Hard on you
We will send you
To live in oblivion.

We will push you away
To suffer in silence
Till we need you again.
Then it starts
All over again!

A Path Misled

I am lost
Without a doubt
This path I'm on
Was abandoned
By society long ago
Always told
Which path to follow
When you know
Deep down
It's just not right.

Instead of letting you
Find out for yourself
What is right or wrong

Why can't they
Just let you follow
The path that is right for you.

BUT you ARE
Different!
They echo.

THAT'S just not true,
I AM ME.

Safety in the Darkness

The room is dark.
There are many doors.
Stumbling through one,
Falling to the floor.

The light intense,
The noise too loud,
Scrambling away,
Heading back.

DARKNESS!
COMFORT!
SAFE!

Try again!
Tomorrow!

DOUBT!!

Crowded Conversation

People ask me,
Why can't you follow
What I am saying
When we are in a
Group conversation?

WELL!

When I walk into
A room full of people,

I can SEE everything,
I can HEAR everything,
I can SMELL everything,

Every conversation,
The clink of a glass
The smell of smoke
From outside the room.

What I can't do,
Is block it all out,
Like you seem to do.
The giggle and laughter,
The heat from other people,
The whispers in the far corner,
Keeping up with the to and fro.

That you seem to know,
Just how to handle.

I sometimes need
A bit more time,
To compile my answers
When trying to keep up with you.

I tend to fumble and stumble
I don't know what to do,
But shut down inside.

Sometimes it is very hard to deal with,
I tend to get exhausted and often
Feel over sensed and nauseated.

The bigger the room,
The larger the crowd,
The worse it gets.
So, I make an excuse and slip away quietly.

Destructive Dreams

Words miss spoken
In the HEAT
Of Conversation,
Can lead to….

Embarrassment,
Frustration,
Angst to try
And explain

Sometimes
My nights of terror
Can deaden my
Mind to the
Ever changing
Surroundings,

I rarely ever tell
Anyone of what
I see,
Experience,
Or encounter in my dreams,

These leave me
Shaking…
Confused…
Nauseated…

These dreams
Have had me
Climbing out windows
Just to escape them
Sometimes I relive them
Night after night.

Mocking laughter
Screeches and being chased,
To whimpers of the ill,
And to HEAT!!!

My emotions,
From day to day
Randomly change
Sometimes without
Warning!!

Often, I am unaware
Until it is too late.

For all of this
I am truly
Sorry!

I struggle each day
Not to end my pain
But I feel I am
A coward.

Train of Conversation

Too many
Complicated questions
With far too
Long an answer.

Flow from the group
I am sitting with.

From Rebuttals
And Replies,
To Queries and Why's.

Restricted Questions!

Ask too personal
A Question,
You lose
Too much ground.

Don't ask a question
You get put down.

Somewhere in
The middle,
Is where
I need to be,
Somewhere
In the middle,
Is where
I cannot see.

Their heads
Are nodding,
Their mouths
Are moving.

Lost to times
Daunting shadow
Intermingling with
This group's
Ever changing mood.

Their voices lost
To the worlds
Surrounding noise.

Normal Life

I can feel
My so called
Normal life
Slowly slipping away
Bit by bit.

As the world
Ever speeds up
Around me.

Trying to grab hold
And hang on
Is a challenge
In itself.

Fantastic Fantasies
Flash before my eyes
And through my mind
As the pressure
Ever increases.

Lost thoughts.

Images long forgotten
Spring forth
With new abundance
Forcing their way
Once more to the surface.

Fighting the ever
Increasing chance
Of insanity
Every day
Leaves me exhausted.

Need some distraction
Television,
Movies,
Computer games.

Anything
Just to dampen
The revolving door
Of life.

New hobbies,
Singing,
Photography,
Writing.

All dampened
By doubt.

Breaking free
Is hard
As I find
Change confusing
Energy sapping
And Frustrating.

Time to venture
Out and try again.

Will see you
On the flip side.

A Day Best Forgotten

Struggle to rise
Keep the sleep from my eyes
Shaking
Uneasy
Jitters taking hold.

This feeling is hard to control
It makes no sense
There was not a murmur
Of a dream
Or nightmare to be had.

Feeling queasy,
Mind has gone numb,
A fog setting in
Words spoken
Get lost in the mist
Of my minds haze.

The day rolls on
Can't seem to sit still for long
Can't talk about
What or how I feel
It is unknown to me.

Too scared to talk to others
Might upset the balance
When asked a question
Mingled jumbled words
Are my reply.

Misused

The needs of the many
Out way
The needs of the few.

The problem is
The few quite often
Get left behind.

Down trodden,

Stepped on,

This phrase was used
In time of war
But in times of peace
It is misused.

We the few
Get pushed to the side
And quite often
Forgotten.

Their reply is
I don't have the time
For just one person.

What they don't
Realise is
**We are
MANY!!**

In My Shoes

You don't know what it feels like
To live inside my shoes.
Have you ever had the words?
Stumble from your lips?

In normal conversation,
Tongue tied,
Despair!

Confused looks reflect back
In utter disbelief.

It is hard to say the words
To someone just like you.

Who seems to know
Just what to say and do.

To make me cringe
And walk away.

Journey's Path

I will climb mountains
Even though there
Are none to be found.

My journey will be rocky
Even though the surface I tread
Is as smooth as glass.

Life at times
Seem far harder
Than it should be.

Obstacles will appear
Out of nowhere
To block my path

People say in general terms
"Life sucks, move on"
Easier said than done,
When those obstacles
Keep moving
To block my path.

Diamond in Disguise

I had a dream last night
Of an angel taking flight
As she lifted off the ground
My eyes widened in surprise.

Hair that flowed like liquid silk
A heart-warming smile
Eyes that sparkled
Like diamonds in the light.

She turned, smiled
And took my hand
Come fly with me
Through the night.

We will soar through the clouds
Let the breeze brush our cheeks
When the breeze becomes too cold.

We will soar down to the lake
And in the golden moonlight
We will leave a rippling wake
Like diamonds sparkling in the night.

When the first glow of light
Reached out to touch her face
My angel started to fade from sight.

Her softly spoken voice
Echoed in my ear
Come fly with me through the night.

As my eyes opened wide
To my surprise
There lay my angel
Bathed in the light
Of the early morning sun.

Dreams and Wishes

Through the bleakness
And days of utter chaos
Darkness of this ever-changing world

Focus on your dreams
As they are yours
And yours alone

Don't let society
Dictate to you
What dreams
You should follow

Try to fight
Through the cloud of doubt
That is often brought on
By an underlying condition

Use this to strengthen
Your dreams
Though at times
This is hard to do

TO THIS I SAY!!

Keep fighting the demons
Who in turn will try
To keep you down.

They will raise
Their ugly heads
When you least
Expect them too.

Find a way
To beat them back
From whence they came.

This is often
Easier said than done.

Your life is yours
And yours alone.

www.ingramcontent.com/pod-product-compliance
Lightning Source LLC
Chambersburg PA
CBHW060344080526
44584CB00013B/907